delicious.

Indulge

Welcome

I'm one of those people who tends to look at the dessert menu before deciding on the main course at a restaurant, and it's just as important when I'm entertaining at home.

Finish a dinner party or special occasion with something spectacular, such as a bread-and-butter pudding with chocolate and rum, or a sticky toffee tart with caramel sauce, and you're guaranteed each guest will go home with a smile on their face.

We've gathered 60 of our all-time favourite sweet recipes, including plenty of classic cakes, luscious ice creams and even no-cook options. I'm sure that these easy-to-follow recipes will be ones you'll turn to whenever the time is right to *Indulge*.

Happy cooking!

Valli

Contents

Cakes and Pastry

Chilled Desserts

Ice Cream

Cheat's chocolate caramel tarts

1 quantity chocolate pastry or
   300g packet dark chocolate
   shortcrust pastry*
200g good-quality dark
   chocolate, chopped
450g jar dulce de leche*
sea salt flakes, to sprinkle

Chocolate pastry
1⅓ cups (200g) plain flour
2 tbs cocoa powder
40g icing sugar
125g chilled unsalted butter,
   chopped
1 egg yolk

If making pastry, whiz the flour, cocoa and sugar in a processor until combined. Add the butter and process to fine crumbs. Add the yolk and 2 tsp chilled water and process until the pastry comes together in a smooth ball. Enclose in plastic wrap. Chill for 30 minutes before rolling out.

Preheat the oven to 180°C. Lightly grease six 10cm loose-bottomed tart pans.

Roll out the pastry to 5mm thick if using homemade. Use the pastry to line the tart pans, trimming the excess. Chill the tart shells for 10 minutes.

Line the tart shells with baking paper and fill with pastry weights or uncooked rice, then bake for 7 minutes. Remove the paper and weights, then return to the oven for a further 2 minutes or until the pastry is crisp and dry. Cool completely in the pans.

Place the chocolate in a heatproof bowl over a saucepan of gently simmering water (don't let the bowl touch the water), stirring until melted and smooth. Remove from the heat and cool slightly.

Use a palette knife to spread the dulce de leche in the tart shells, then pour over the chocolate, gently swirling the tart to completely cover the caramel. Cool at room temperature until set.

Once set, sprinkle each tart with the sea salt and serve. **Makes 6**

* We used Careme Dark Chocolate Shortcrust Pastry. For stockists, visit: caremepastry.com. Dulce de leche is a South American milk caramel available from gourmet food shops.

Self-saucing chocolate pudding

60g unsalted butter

½ cup (125ml) milk

1 tsp vanilla extract

¾ cup (165g) caster sugar

1 cup (150g) self-raising flour,
   sifted

2 tbs cocoa powder, sifted,
   plus extra to dust

¾ firmly packed cup (185g)
   brown sugar

Thick cream, to serve

Preheat the oven to 180°C. Grease a 1.5-litre (6-cup) ovenproof baking dish.

Melt the butter with the milk in a saucepan over low heat. Add the vanilla, caster sugar, flour and 1 tablespoon cocoa, stirring to combine, then spread into the baking dish.

Combine the brown sugar and remaining 1 tablespoon cocoa in a bowl with 2 cups (500ml) boiling water. Stir until sugar has dissolved, then carefully pour over the pudding batter. Bake for 35–40 minutes until the top is firm. Stand for 5 minutes.

Dust with the extra cocoa and serve with the thick cream.

Serves 4–6

Baci biscuits

40g unsalted butter, softened
1 egg
400g jar Nutella or other
   chocolate hazelnut spread
1¼ cups (185g) self-raising
   flour, sifted
Cocoa powder, to serve

Preheat the oven to 180°C. Line 2 large baking trays with baking paper.

Place the butter, egg and ¾ cup (235g) Nutella in a bowl and beat with electric beaters for 2–3 minutes until thick. Gradually add the flour, beating constantly, until you have a sticky dough.

Using floured hands, roll 1 teaspoon dough into a ball. Repeat until you have 50 balls. Place on the baking trays, spaced 2cm apart, and bake for 6–7 minutes until firm to the touch. Transfer to a wire rack to cool completely.

Spread the remaining Nutella on 25 biscuits, then sandwich with the remaining 25 biscuits. Serve dusted with the cocoa. These biscuits will keep in an airtight container for up to 3 days. **Makes 25**

Little black dress chocolate cake

500g good-quality dark
  chocolate, chopped
125g unsalted butter,
  chopped
6 eggs, separated
90g caster sugar
150ml thickened cream
2 tbs dark rum or brandy
1 tsp vanilla extract
½ tsp cream of tartar
Edible silver or gold leaf*,
  to serve

Chocolate ganache
450g good-quality dark
  chocolate, chopped
175g unsalted butter
600ml thickened cream
¼ cup (90g) liquid glucose*

Preheat the oven to 180°C. Grease a 24cm springform cake pan and line the base with baking paper.

Place the chocolate and butter in a heatproof bowl set over a saucepan of gently simmering water (don't let the bowl touch the water). Stir until the mixture is smooth and combined, then remove the bowl from the heat and set aside to cool slightly.

Place the egg yolks and sugar in an electric mixer and beat until thick and pale. Stir in the cream, rum or brandy, vanilla and cooled chocolate mixture.

Whisk the eggwhites and cream of tartar in a large, clean, dry bowl until soft peaks form. In 3 batches, gently fold the eggwhite into the chocolate mixture with a metal spoon, trying to keep as much air in the mixture as possible. Spread into the prepared pan and bake for 25 minutes until a skewer inserted into the centre comes out with a few moist crumbs attached. Cool completely in the pan on a wire rack.

To make the chocolate ganache, place the chocolate and butter in a bowl set over a pan of simmering water (don't let the bowl touch the water), stirring until smooth. Remove from heat.

Place the cream and glucose in a pan, bring to just below boiling point. Pour over the chocolate mixture and stir until smooth. Chill for 30 minutes or until thick.

Run a knife around the edge of the cake to remove from the pan. Gently reheat the ganache and spread over the cooled cake and garnish with the silver or gold leaf. **Serves 8–10**

* Liquid glucose is from supermarkets. Edible silver and gold leaf are from cake decorating shops and stationery shops.

Mars bar trifle

6 gold-strength gelatine
   leaves*
250g caster sugar
30g cocoa powder
100ml Pedro Ximénez sherry*
   or Marsala*
12 sponge finger biscuits
   (savoiardi) (about 120g),
   broken into pieces
4 x 60g Mars bars
350ml milk
300ml thickened cream,
   whipped

Soak 4 gelatine leaves in cold water for 5 minutes to soften.

Meanwhile, place the sugar and 1 cup (250ml) water in a saucepan over low heat, stirring to dissolve the sugar. Increase the heat to medium and simmer for 4 minutes until thickened slightly, then whisk in the cocoa.

Squeeze the excess water from the gelatine leaves and add the leaves to the syrup, stirring to dissolve. Add the sherry or Marsala and mix well. Strain and set aside to cool slightly.

Place the biscuits in a trifle bowl. Pour over the cocoa syrup, pressing the biscuits down well. Cover and chill in the fridge for 2–3 hours to set.

For the second layer, soak the remaining 2 gelatine leaves in cold water for 5 minutes until softened. Meanwhile, chop 3 Mars bars and place in a saucepan with the milk over low heat, stirring until melted and smooth. Squeeze excess water from the gelatine, then add the leaves to the milk mixture and stir to dissolve. Cool slightly, then pour over the chilled layer and return to the fridge for 1–2 hours until set.

To serve, spread the whipped cream over the trifle, then top with remaining sliced Mars bar. **Serves 4–6**

* Gelatine leaves are available from gourmet food shops – check the packet for setting instructions. Pedro Ximénez (a sweet, sticky Spanish sherry) and Marsala (an Italian fortified wine) are available from selected bottle shops.

Dulce de leche brownies

200g dark chocolate,
  chopped
250g unsalted butter,
  chopped
1¾ firmly packed cups
  (385g) brown sugar
4 eggs
1⅓ cups (200g) plain flour
¼ tsp baking powder
⅓ cup (35g) good-quality
  cocoa powder
450g jar dulce de leche*

Preheat the oven to 180°C. Grease a 22cm square cake pan and line with baking paper, leaving plenty overhanging the sides.

Place the chocolate and butter in a small saucepan over low heat and stir until melted and smooth. Transfer to a bowl and stir in the brown sugar and eggs. Sift in the flour, baking powder and cocoa and stir gently to combine. Pour half the mixture into the prepared pan.

Dollop 8 teaspoonfuls of dulce de leche over the batter in the pan. Use a wooden skewer to gently swirl the caramel over the chocolate (but don't cut through the mixture, as this will spoil the brownies). Spread the remaining batter over the top and repeat with another 8 teaspoonfuls of the dulce de leche.

Bake for 35–40 minutes or until set (the dulce de leche will still be molten). Remove from the oven and allow to cool slightly. Run a knife around the edge of the pan to loosen, then use the baking paper to ease the slice out of the pan. Cut into 12 squares and serve warm or cold with the remaining dulce de leche to dollop.
Makes 12

* Ready-made dulce de leche (South American milk caramel) is available from gourmet food shops and delis.

Chocolate lava puddings

250g unsalted butter, softened

1 firmly packed cup (250g) brown sugar

4 eggs

1 cup (150g) plain flour

½ cup (50g) cocoa powder

6 chocolate truffles (such as Lindt Lindor balls), chilled

Icing sugar and pure (thin) cream or ice cream, to serve

Preheat the oven to 180°C and grease six ¾ cup (185ml) ramekins.

Place the butter and brown sugar in a bowl and beat with electric beaters until thick and pale. Add the eggs, 1 at a time, beating well after each addition. Sift in the flour and cocoa, then fold gently with a metal spoon until just combined.

Divide half the pudding batter among the ramekins, then place a truffle in the centre of each. Top with the remaining pudding batter, then bake for 20 minutes or until just firm to the touch.

Stand the puddings for 5 minutes, then dust with the icing sugar and serve with the cream or ice cream. **Serves 6**

Chocolate hazelnut tart

300g packet dark chocolate
   shortcrust pastry* or
   1 quantity chocolate pastry
   (page 6)
1 cup (250ml) thickened
   cream
60g unsalted butter, chopped
¼ cup (60ml) light corn
   syrup* or glucose syrup*
1 cup (220g) caster sugar
2⅓ cups (350g) hazelnuts,
   toasted, skins removed
50g dark chocolate, chopped

Roll out the pastry to 5mm thick, then use to line a 28cm loose-bottomed tart pan. Chill for 30 minutes.

Preheat the oven to 180°C.

Line the pastry with baking paper, and weigh down with pastry weights or uncooked rice. Blind-bake for 10 minutes, then remove paper and weights and return to the oven for a further 5 minutes until dry. Leave to cool while you make the filling.

Place the cream and butter in a saucepan over medium heat and bring to just below boiling point. Remove from the heat and set aside.

Place the corn or glucose syrup and ⅓ cup (80ml) water in a separate saucepan, then sprinkle with the sugar. Place over medium heat and cook, stirring occasionally, until the sugar has dissolved and the liquid is clear. Increase the heat to high and cook, without stirring, until a golden honey colour. Remove from the heat, then carefully whisk the cream mixture into the toffee. Return the pan to low heat and stir to dissolve any hard bits of toffee. Add the nuts and cook for 1 minute. Pour the mixture into the tart shell and bake for 17–20 minutes until the tart filling is firm. Remove from the oven and allow to cool.

Just before serving, melt the chocolate in a heatproof bowl set over a saucepan of simmering water (don't let the bowl touch the water). Use a spoon to quickly drizzle the chocolate back and forth over the tart. Alternatively, place the melted chocolate in a snap-lock bag, snip off one corner of the bag, then drizzle over the tart. **Serves 6–8**

* We used Careme Dark Chocolate Shortcrust Pastry. For stockists, visit caremepastry.com. Light corn syrup and glucose syrup are from the baking aisle in supermarkets.

Profiteroles with ice cream and chocolate sauce

300ml good-quality vanilla
  ice cream
30 store-bought profiteroles*,
  split
250g good-quality dark
  chocolate, roughly
  chopped
½ cup (125ml) thickened
  cream
Splash of Cognac or brandy

Allow the ice cream to soften in the fridge for 30 minutes. Sandwich each profiterole with a scoop of softened ice cream, then return to the freezer on a tray as you go. This can be done up to a week in advance.

When almost ready to serve, place the chocolate, cream and alcohol in a saucepan over low heat until the chocolate has melted. Stir gently to combine, then serve the warm sauce drizzled over the profiteroles. **Makes 30**

* From Italian grocers and selected supermarkets.

Chocolate caramel slice

250g digestive or shortbread
   biscuits
70g unsalted butter, melted
1 cup (250ml) thickened
   cream
250g can caramel Top 'N' Fill
250g good-quality dark
   chocolate, chopped
4 egg yolks
1 tbs olive oil

Grease a 26cm x 18cm lamington pan and line with baking paper, leaving some overhanging the sides.

Crush the biscuits in a food processor, then add the butter and pulse to combine well. Press into the base of the pan and chill for about 15 minutes until firm.

Place the cream and caramel in a saucepan and stir over low heat until combined and heated through. Remove from the heat, add 120g chocolate and stir until smooth.

Whisk the egg yolks in a bowl, then gradually whisk in the hot cream mixture. Pour the mixture over the biscuit base, then chill for about 2–3 hours until cooled and set.

Place the remaining chocolate and the oil in a heatproof bowl set over a saucepan of simmering water (don't let the bowl touch the water) and stir until melted and smooth. Set aside to cool. Pour over the base and chill for 30 minutes or until set.

Use the overhanging baking paper to carefully lift the slice from the pan. Use a hot knife (dipped in hot water) to cut the slice into 12 bars. Keep in an airtight container in the fridge for up to 2 days.
Makes 12

Refrigerator cake

150g pitted prunes, roughly chopped

⅓ cup (80ml) Pedro Ximénez sherry*, plus extra to serve

250g digestive biscuits, roughly chopped

100g raw pecans, chopped

100g unsalted pistachios, chopped

15 (about 50g) glacé cherries

150g unsalted butter, chopped

5 tbs golden syrup

500g dark chocolate, chopped

Cocoa powder, to dust

Line a 25cm x 10cm loaf pan with plastic wrap, leaving some overhanging the sides to cover.

Place the prunes and sherry in a small bowl and leave to soak for 2–3 hours.

Combine the biscuits, nuts and glacé cherries in a bowl.

Place the butter, golden syrup and chocolate in a heatproof bowl over a saucepan of simmering water (don't let the bowl touch the water), stirring gently, until the chocolate melts. Remove from the heat. Add the biscuit mixture, prunes and any soaking liquid, stirring to combine. Press the mixture down well into the loaf pan to expel any air bubbles, cover with the overhanging plastic wrap and chill for at least 4 hours, preferably overnight, until set.

Invert onto a platter and dust with the cocoa just before serving. Cut into 2cm-thick slices and serve with small glasses of sherry. Keep in an airtight container in the fridge for up to 1 week.

Serves 8–10

* Pedro Ximénez is a sweet, sticky Spanish sherry, available from selected bottle shops.

Classic chocolate pots

½ cup (125ml) pure (thin)
   cream, plus whipped cream
   to serve
½ cup (125ml) milk
100g good-quality dark
   chocolate, chopped, plus
   extra shaved to sprinkle
3 egg yolks
2 tbs caster sugar
1 tsp vanilla extract

Preheat the oven to 160°C.

Place the cream and milk in a saucepan over medium-low heat and bring to just below boiling point. Add the chocolate and stir until just melted, then remove from the heat.

Whisk the egg yolks, sugar and vanilla in a bowl until just combined. Gradually whisk in the chocolate mixture, combining well. Strain into a jug, then pour into four 200ml heatproof serving glasses or ramekins. Place in a roasting pan and pour in enough hot water to come halfway up the sides of the glasses or ramekins.

Bake for 25 minutes or until just set with a slight wobble. Remove from the water bath and set aside to cool. Chill for at least 4 hours or until ready to serve.

Serve the chocolate pots topped with the whipped cream and shaved chocolate. **Makes 4**

Sticky mocha puddings with chocolate and toffee sauce

1 cup (170g) pitted dates
1 tsp bicarbonate of soda
90g unsalted butter, softened
125g brown sugar
2 tsp vanilla extract
2 eggs, beaten
175g plain flour
2 tsp baking powder
2 tsp coffee essence*
200g dark chocolate, finely
    chopped
Vanilla or hazelnut ice cream,
    to serve

Sauce
175g brown sugar
125g unsalted butter
150ml thickened cream
50g dark chocolate, chopped

Preheat the oven to 180°C. Grease a 24cm round cake pan and line with baking paper.

Place the dates and soda in a bowl and pour over 175ml boiling water. Set aside for 30 minutes to soften.

Meanwhile, beat the butter, sugar and vanilla together with electric beaters until thick and pale. Add the eggs and beat until well combined.

Place the date mixture and the soaking liquid in a food processor and process until smooth, then add to the cake mixture. Fold in the flour, baking powder, coffee essence and chopped chocolate. Spread into the cake pan, then bake for 45–50 minutes until a skewer inserted in the centre comes out clean. Allow to rest in the pan for 15 minutes before turning out onto a wire rack to cool.

Meanwhile, for the chocolate sauce, place all of the ingredients in a saucepan and stir over low heat for 2–3 minutes until smooth.

Slice the cake and serve with the ice cream, drizzled with the warm chocolate sauce. **Serves 6–8**

* Coffee essence is available from supermarkets.

Yin-yang chocolate cake

250g unsalted butter, chopped
250g good-quality dark chocolate, chopped
4 eggs, separated
½ cup (110g) caster sugar
½ firmly packed cup (110g) brown sugar
⅓ cup (50g) plain flour
50g almond meal
Cocoa powder, to dust
Icing sugar, to dust

Preheat the oven to 170°C and grease and line a 23cm springform cake pan.

Melt the butter and chocolate in a heatproof bowl set over a saucepan of gently simmering water (don't let the bowl touch the water). Cool slightly.

In a large bowl, whisk the egg yolks, caster sugar and brown sugar with electric beaters until thick and pale. Stir in the cooled chocolate mixture, then fold in the flour and almond meal.

In a large, clean bowl, whisk the eggwhites with a pinch of salt until soft peaks form, then gently fold into the cake mixture, taking care to keep as much air in the mixture as possible. Pour into the prepared pan, then bake for 30 minutes. The cake will still be a little moist in the centre but will firm on cooling. Cool in the pan for 10 minutes, then transfer to a wire rack to cool completely.

To make the yin-yang template, cut a 23cm circle of baking paper, then draw an S-shape down the centre to create 2 large 'commas'. Using a 20-cent coin as a guide, draw a circle on one side. Cut out the comma and circle to create half a yin-yang symbol. Place the template on one side of the cake and dust generously with the cocoa. Shake the template clean, then place on the opposite side and dust liberally with the icing sugar. **Serves 6–8**

Chocolate-chip tiramisu

6 eggs, separated
400g caster sugar
1kg mascarpone
200g dark chocolate
200ml strong espresso
¾ firmly packed cup (185g)
  brown sugar
200ml Kahlua or other coffee
  liqueur
2 tbs cocoa powder, plus
  extra to dust
36 sponge finger biscuits
  (savoiardi)

Place the egg yolks and 200g caster sugar in a heatproof bowl set over a saucepan of simmering water (don't let the bowl touch the water). Whisk until thick and pale, then remove from the heat and set aside to cool.

Gradually beat the mascarpone into the cooled egg yolk mixture until smooth and well combined. Finely chop 150g chocolate and fold into the mascarpone mixture. Set aside.

In a clean, dry bowl, whisk the eggwhites until soft peaks form. Gradually add the remaining 200g caster sugar, whisking until stiff and glossy, then fold into the mascarpone mixture.

Combine the espresso, brown sugar, Kahlua and cocoa in a saucepan. Stir over low heat until the sugar has dissolved, then remove from the heat and allow to cool.

Dip 12 sponge fingers into the espresso mixture, then arrange in a 20cm square loose-bottomed cake pan or a 1.5-litre (6-cup) serving dish, cutting the sponge fingers to fit. Spread with one-third of the mascarpone mixture. Repeat the layers twice more, alternating the direction of the sponge fingers – this will help keep the tiramisu stable. Cover and chill for at least 4 hours or overnight.

To serve, shave the remaining 50g chocolate into shards using a vegetable peeler and scatter over the tiramisu. Dust with the extra cocoa and cut into slices. **Serves 8–10**

Steamed blueberry pudding

125g unsalted butter,
   softened
125g caster sugar
1 tsp vanilla extract
4 eggs
1⅔ cups (250g) self-raising
   flour, sifted
Finely grated zest of ½ lemon
⅓ cup (80ml) milk
½ cup (160g) blueberry jam
125g fresh or frozen
   blueberries
Pure (thin) cream, to serve

Preheat the oven to 180°C and grease a 1.25-litre (5-cup) pudding basin.

Beat the butter, sugar and vanilla in an electric mixer until pale and thick. Add the eggs one at a time, beating well after each addition. Fold in the flour and lemon zest, followed by the milk until combined (the mixture should be a soft dropping consistency).

Spread half each of the jam and berries in the base of the pudding basin, then pour in the batter. Layer a sheet of foil on top of a sheet of baking paper, then fold a pleat through the centre. Use to cover the pudding, then tie with kitchen string. Place in a roasting pan, then fill the pan with enough boiling water to come halfway up the sides of the basin. Cook in the oven for 1 hour 15 minutes or until a skewer inserted in the centre comes out clean. Stand for 5 minutes.

Meanwhile, warm the remaining jam with the berries over low heat for 2–3 minutes to make a warm sauce.

Turn the pudding out onto a platter, then drizzle with the warm sauce and the chilled cream to serve. **Serves 4–6**

Sticky date tart with toffee sauce

1½ cups (240g) pitted dates,
 chopped into small pieces
150ml milk
1 tsp bicarbonate of soda
1 quantity sweet shortcrust
 pastry or 435g packet
 Careme Vanilla Bean Sweet
 Shortcrust Pastry*
1 tsp vanilla extract
⅔ cup (100g) plain flour,
 sifted
2 eggs, lightly beaten
2 tbs golden syrup
100g brown sugar
¼ cup (20g) flaked almonds
Icing sugar, to dust

Sweet shortcrust pastry
1⅔ cups (250g) plain flour
2 tbs icing sugar
1 vanilla bean, split
 lengthways, seeds scraped
180g chilled unsalted butter,
 chopped
1 egg yolk

Toffee sauce
200g brown sugar
50g unsalted butter
300ml thickened cream

If making pastry, process the flour, icing sugar, vanilla seeds and a pinch of salt in a food processor until there are no lumps. Add the butter and process until you have fine crumbs. Add the yolk and 1 tablespoon chilled water, then process until the mixture comes together in a smooth ball. Enclose in plastic wrap, then chill for 1 hour.

Place the dates and milk in a saucepan over medium heat. Bring to just below boiling point, then remove from the heat. Stir in the bicarbonate of soda, then stand for 30 minutes or until the dates have softened.

Meanwhile, roll out the homemade or bought pastry to 5mm thick. Use the pastry to line a greased 36cm x 12cm rectangular loose-bottomed tart pan, trimming the excess. Chill for 10 minutes.

Preheat the oven to 180°C.

Line the tart case with baking paper and fill with pastry weights or uncooked rice. Bake for 8 minutes. Remove the paper and weights, then bake for a further 2–3 minutes until golden and dry.

Reduce the oven to 160°C.

Place the dates and milk in a food processor with the vanilla and pulse to combine. Transfer to a bowl, then fold in the flour, eggs, golden syrup and brown sugar until just combined. Set aside.

For the toffee sauce, place all the ingredients in a saucepan over low heat, stirring until the sugar dissolves. Cook for 2 minutes or until slightly thickened.

Pour ⅓ cup (80ml) toffee sauce in the tart shell, then spread the date mixture on top and scatter with the almonds. Bake for 20–25 minutes until just set. Cool in the pan for 5 minutes.

Remove the sticky date tart from the pan and dust with the icing sugar. Cut into slices and serve warm with the remaining toffee sauce. **Serves 6**

* For stockists, visit: caremepastry.com.

Apple and passionfruit crumble

130g chilled unsalted butter, chopped
8 green apples, peeled, sliced
⅔ cup (150g) caster sugar
Pulp of 8 passionfruit
1 tsp vanilla extract
1⅓ cups (200g) plain flour
Custard, to serve

Custard
5 egg yolks
¼ cup (55g) caster sugar
2 cups (500ml) pure (thin) cream
1 vanilla bean, split lengthways, seeds scraped

To make the custard, gently whisk the egg yolks and sugar together to combine. Set aside.

Place the cream and vanilla pod and seeds in a saucepan over medium heat and bring to just below boiling point. Remove from heat and cool slightly, then whisk the cream mixture into the egg mixture until combined.

Return the custard to a clean saucepan over low heat. Cook for 5–6 minutes, stirring constantly, until thick enough to coat the back of the spoon.

Strain the custard into a jug, then cover the surface closely with plastic wrap to prevent a skin from forming.

Preheat the oven to 180°C and grease six ¾ cup (185ml) ramekins or ovenproof cups (or use a 1-litre/4-cup baking dish).

Place 30g butter in a saucepan over medium-low heat. Add the apple, 40g sugar and ¼ cup (60ml) water, then cook for 5–6 minutes until softened. Stir in the passionfruit and vanilla, then divide among the ramekins or cups.

Place the flour and remaining ½ cup (110g) sugar and 100g butter in a food processor and whiz to coarse crumbs. Scatter the crumbs over the apple mixture, then bake for 35–40 minutes until golden and bubbling. Gently reheat the custard and serve the crumble warm with the custard. **Serves 6**

Jam and chocolate roly poly with proper custard

1 cup (150g) self-raising flour
2 tbs caster sugar
75g powdered suet mix*
100ml milk
1 cup (320g) raspberry jam
½ cup (90g) chopped
   dark chocolate
Custard (see page 40), to
   serve

Sift the flour into a bowl, then stir in the sugar, suet and ½ teaspoon salt. Add the milk and stir to form a soft dough.

On a lightly floured surface, roll the dough out to a 20cm x 30cm rectangle. Spread with the jam, leaving a 2cm border on all sides. Scatter with the chocolate, then roll up tightly from the long side to form a long roll.

Lightly grease a sheet of baking paper, then place the roly poly, seam-side down, on the baking paper. Fold in the ends and tuck underneath the roll. Wrap in foil, twisting the ends to seal.

Place the roly poly in a large steamer or fish kettle and steam for 45 minutes, topping up the water, if necessary. To test if it's cooked, pull back the foil and baking paper – the roly poly should spring back when lightly touched. Remove from the steamer and stand for 10 minutes.

Remove the foil and baking paper from the roly poly and cut into thick slices. Serve with the warm custard. **Serves 6–8**

* Powdered suet mix is available from the baking aisle in supermarkets.

Rhubarb and strawberry crumble with creme anglaise

1 bunch rhubarb

250g strawberries, halved
   if large

1 vanilla bean, split
   lengthways, seeds scraped

Grated zest and juice of
   1 orange

¼ cup (55g) demerara or raw
   sugar

300ml creme anglaise
   (see page 52)

Crumble

2 tbs self-raising flour

2 tbs demerara or raw sugar

¼ cup (25g) walnuts, toasted,
   chopped

20g unsalted butter, chilled

Preheat the oven to 180°C and line a baking tray with baking paper.

Trim the rhubarb, then cut into 8cm pieces. Place the rhubarb in a baking dish in a single layer, then scatter with the strawberries, vanilla bean and seeds, orange zest and juice and sugar. Cover with foil and bake for 15–20 minutes or until tender but the rhubarb is holding its shape. Discard the vanilla bean.

Meanwhile for the crumble, place the flour in a food processor with the sugar and walnuts. Pulse once or twice to combine, then add the butter and pulse until the mixture comes together in clumps. Spread the crumble mixture onto the lined tray and bake for 15 minutes, stirring once, until golden. Remove from the oven and allow to cool slightly, then break up any large clumps with your fingers.

Pour the creme anglaise into 4 glasses, top with the rhubarb and strawberries, then scatter with the crumble mixture and serve.

Serves 4

Chocolate and rum bread and butter pudding

½ cup (80g) sultanas

⅓ cup (80ml) dark rum

300g brioche loaf*,
    thinly sliced

60g unsalted butter, softened

100g dark chocolate,
    chopped

4 eggs

½ cup (110g) caster sugar

300ml pure (thin) cream, plus
    extra to serve

½ cup (125ml) milk

1 tsp vanilla extract

Icing sugar, to dust

Grease a 1.5-litre (6-cup) ceramic baking dish. Place the sultanas and rum in a bowl and stand for 30 minutes.

Spread one side of each brioche slice with the butter. Arrange half the brioche in the baking dish, buttered-side up, and sprinkle with half each of the chocolate, soaked sultanas and soaking rum. Repeat the layers.

Whisk the eggs, sugar, cream, milk and vanilla together in a bowl until combined. Strain, then pour over the pudding. Stand for 30 minutes to allow the egg mixture to soak into the brioche and the flavours to develop.

Preheat the oven to 170°C.

Place the pudding in a deep roasting pan. Pour enough boiling water into the pan to come halfway up the side of the baking dish. Bake for 1 hour or until the custard has set (cover loosely with foil if the pudding is browning too quickly). Remove the pudding from the roasting pan and stand for 10 minutes.

Dust with the icing sugar and serve with the extra cream.

Serves 6–8

* Brioche is from selected supermarkets or order from your baker.

Cherry clafoutis

½ cup (75g) plain flour
600ml pure (thin) cream,
   plus extra whipped cream
   to serve
5 eggs plus extra 7 egg yolks
1½ cups (330g) caster sugar
670g jar morello cherries in
   syrup, drained, syrup
   reserved
1 vanilla bean, split
   lengthways, seeds scraped

Whisk the flour, cream, eggs, egg yolks and 1 cup (220g) sugar together until smooth. Stand the batter at room temperature for 1 hour.

Meanwhile, place the reserved cherry syrup, vanilla bean and seeds, and remaining ½ cup (110g) sugar in a saucepan over low heat, stirring until the sugar dissolves. Increase the heat to medium and simmer for 5 minutes or until reduced and syrupy. Allow to cool, then remove the vanilla bean.

Preheat the oven to 160°C and grease a 2-litre (8-cup) baking dish.

Place the drained cherries in the baking dish, then pour over the batter. Bake for 1 hour or until puffed and golden. Cool in the dish for 10 minutes.

Cut the clafoutis into squares and serve warm with the whipped cream and the vanilla and cherry syrup. **Serves 6–8**

Little mandarin puddings

90g caster sugar,
  plus extra to sprinkle
2 mandarins, sliced into
  rounds, plus thinly
  zested rind and juice
  of 1 mandarin
90g unsalted butter, softened
90g self-raising flour
½ tsp baking powder
2 eggs
1½ tbs sour cream
1 tbs orange marmalade
½ tsp ground ginger
½ tsp ground cinnamon
2 tsp golden syrup
Pure (thin) cream or custard
  (see page 40), to serve

Mandarin syrup
⅓ cup (75g) caster sugar
Juice of 2 mandarins
2 tbs golden syrup

Preheat the oven to 180°C. Grease six 1-cup (250ml) dariole moulds and sprinkle the insides with the extra caster sugar, shaking out any excess. Line the base of each dariole mould with a mandarin round.

Place the butter and sugar in a bowl and beat with electric beaters until thick and pale. Add the flour, baking powder, eggs, sour cream, marmalade, spices, golden syrup and mandarin juice, then beat for a further 2–3 minutes until combined.

Divide the pudding batter among the moulds. Place a small sheet of foil on a small sheet of baking paper, then fold a pleat through the centre. Use to cover a mould, baking paper-side down, and secure with kitchen string. Repeat for the remaining moulds.

Place the moulds in a roasting pan, then pour enough boiling water into the pan to come halfway up the sides of the moulds. Bake for 55–60 minutes until a skewer inserted in the centre comes out clean.

Meanwhile, place the mandarin rind in a saucepan over low heat and cover with cold water. Simmer for 10 minutes. Drain. Repeat the blanching method 2 more times. (This will remove the bitterness from the rind.)

For the mandarin syrup, place the sugar, mandarin juice and golden syrup in a saucepan over low heat, stirring to dissolve the sugar. Increase the heat to medium and simmer for 3–4 minutes until reduced and syrupy.

Invert the puddings onto serving plates and pour over the syrup. Garnish with the blanched mandarin rind and serve with the cream or custard. **Serves 6**

Peach and ginger crumble

2 x 400g cans sliced peaches
   in natural juice
2 tbs chopped stem ginger
   in syrup*
300g good-quality ginger
   biscuits*
60g unsalted butter, softened
Creme anglaise (see below)
   or pure (thin) cream, to
   serve

Creme anglaise
5 egg yolks
2 cups (500ml) pure (thin)
   cream
¼ cup (55g) caster sugar
1 vanilla bean, split
   lengthways, seeds scraped

Preheat the oven to 170°C.

Drain the peach slices, reserving ½ cup (125ml) of the juice. Combine the peach slices, reserved juice and the stem ginger in a bowl, then transfer to a shallow 1.5-litre (6-cup) baking dish.

Place the biscuits in a food processor and process to fine crumbs. Add the butter and pulse until the mixture resembles coarse breadcrumbs.

Cover the peaches with the crumble mixture, then bake for 20 minutes or until golden and bubbling.

While the crumble is baking, make the creme anglaise. Gently whisk the egg yolks and caster sugar in a bowl until combined. Place the cream and the vanilla pod and seeds in a pan over medium heat and bring to just below boiling point. Pour the cream over the egg mixture, whisking gently to combine.

Return the custard mixture to a clean pan and place over very low heat. Stir with a wooden spoon for 5–6 minutes until the mixture thickens and coats the back of the spoon – watch carefully as you don't want to scramble the eggs. (If it does curdle, I've had success with the method used to rescue hollandaise: put everything, except the vanilla bean, in a blender, add an ice cube, then blend well. Keep your fingers crossed.) Strain into a jug.

Serve the crumble with the warm (or chilled) creme anglaise or cream. **Serves 6**

* Stem ginger in syrup is available from selected supermarkets and delis. We used ginger shortbread.

Limoncello soufflé

Melted butter, to brush

¼ cup (55g) caster sugar, plus extra to dust

6 eggwhites

Pinch of cream of tartar

325g jar good-quality lemon curd*

Grated zest of 1 lemon

2 tbs limoncello*, plus extra chilled to serve

Icing sugar, to dust

Preheat the oven to 200°C. Brush eight 150ml soufflé dishes or ramekins with melted butter. Dust with a little extra caster sugar, tapping to remove excess.

Use electric beaters to whisk the eggwhites and cream of tartar until soft peaks form. Gradually add the sugar, beating constantly, until the mixture is stiff and glossy.

Meanwhile, gently warm the curd and zest in a saucepan over low heat. Stir in the limoncello, then transfer to a large bowl. Use a large metal spoon to gently fold one-third of the eggwhites into the lemon mixture. Continue to fold in the remaining eggwhites until just combined, taking care not to lose too much volume. Divide among the ramekins and run your finger around the inside edge of each ramekin. Bake for 12 minutes or until golden and risen. Dust with the icing sugar, then serve immediately with the extra chilled limoncello. **Makes 8**

* Good-quality lemon curd is from gourmet food shops and delis. Limoncello is an Italian-style lemon liqueur available from selected bottle shops.

Coconut pancakes with banana and creme fraiche

3 ripe bananas

4 eggs, separated

1 cup (250ml) coconut milk

1 cup (150g) plain flour, sifted

1 tsp baking powder, sifted

Melted unsalted butter, to grease

Creme fraiche, caramel sauce, icing sugar and shredded coconut, to serve

Caramel sauce

50g unsalted butter

½ firmly packed cup (100g) brown sugar

3 tbs golden syrup

150ml thickened cream

1 tsp vanilla extract

To make the caramel sauce, place all the ingredients in a pan over low heat, stir to dissolve the sugar, then simmer for 5 minutes until thickened.

Mash 1 banana in a bowl, then set aside.

Place the egg yolks, coconut milk and a pinch of salt in a bowl and whisk until combined. Gently fold in the sifted flour, baking powder and mashed banana until combined.

Whisk the eggwhites in a separate bowl until stiff peaks form, then fold into the batter.

Heat a non-stick frypan over medium-low heat and brush with the melted butter. Using a heaped tablespoon of batter for each pancake, add 3–4 spoonfuls to the pan and cook for 2–3 minutes each side until golden and cooked through. Keep the pancakes warm while you continue with the remaining batter to make a total of 9 pancakes.

Slice the remaining bananas. Arrange the pancakes in stacks on serving plates, alternating each layer with the banana slices and creme fraiche. Drizzle with the caramel sauce (warm or cold), then dust with the icing sugar and sprinkle with the shredded coconut.

Serves 3–4

Strawberry tart with basil cream

200g amaretti (Italian almond
   biscuits)*
125g unsalted butter, melted,
   cooled
2 x 250g punnets
   strawberries, halved if
   large*
2 tbs icing sugar, sifted,
   plus extra to serve
600ml thickened cream
2 tsp finely grated lime zest
Pulp of 2 passionfruit
6 large basil leaves, finely
   chopped
⅓ cup (95g) thick
   Greek-style yoghurt

Grease a 22cm loose-bottomed tart pan.

Place the amaretti in a food processor and whiz to fine crumbs. Add the butter and pulse a few times to combine, then press into the base and side of the tart pan. Chill for 30 minutes to firm up.

Place the strawberries in a bowl and toss with the icing sugar. Set aside.

Place the cream and lime zest in a separate bowl and beat with electric beaters until stiff peaks form. Strain the passionfruit pulp into the cream mixture, pressing down with the back of a spoon to extract as much juice as possible and discarding the seeds, then gently fold to combine. Fold in the basil and yoghurt.

Fill the tart shell with the basil cream and arrange the strawberries on top. Serve the tart dusted with the extra icing sugar.

Serves 6–8

* Available from delis and gourmet food shops. Just for presentation, keep some of the strawberries unhulled. The bright green leaves add an extra burst of colour to this tart.

Meringues with mango mojito sauce

4 eggwhites
250g caster sugar
2 tsp cornflour
1 tsp white wine vinegar
2–3 drops yellow food
  colouring
300ml thickened cream,
  lightly whipped

Mango mojito sauce
2 large mangoes, chopped,
  plus extra mango to serve
¼ cup (60ml) white rum
1 tbs lime juice
1 tbs chopped mint leaves,
  plus extra leaves to serve
⅓ cup (75g) caster sugar

Preheat the oven to 140°C and line a baking tray with baking paper.

Place the eggwhites and sugar in a heatproof bowl set over a saucepan of gently simmering water (don't let the bowl touch the water). Whisk constantly for 6–8 minutes until the sugar has dissolved and the mixture is thick. Transfer to an electric mixer and continue to whisk for 10 minutes or until the meringue mixture is cool, stiff and glossy. Fold in the cornflour and vinegar, then use a skewer to swirl the yellow food colouring through the meringue.

Place 6 dollops of meringue mixture on the baking tray, making a shallow indent in the centre of each with the back of a spoon. Bake for 1 hour, then turn off the oven and allow the meringues to cool completely in the oven with the door slightly ajar.

Meanwhile, for the mango mojito sauce, whiz all the ingredients together in a food processor until smooth.

Top the meringues with the whipped cream, then decorate with the extra mango and mint leaves. Serve drizzled with the mango mojito sauce. The unfilled meringues will keep in an airtight container for up to 2 days. **Serves 6**

Caramel raspberry tarts with orange cream

3 sheets frozen puff pastry,
    thawed
100g brown sugar
50g unsalted butter
300ml thickened cream
2 x 125g punnets raspberries
2 tbs icing sugar, sifted
Finely grated zest of
    1 orange

Preheat the oven to 200°C. Line a baking tray with baking paper.

Using a 10cm round pastry cutter, cut the pastry into 6 rounds. Place the pastry rounds on the baking tray and prick with a fork. Place another sheet of baking paper on top and weigh down the pastry with a heavy baking tray. Bake for 25 minutes or until the pastry is golden.

Meanwhile, place the brown sugar, butter and ¼ cup (60ml) cream in a frypan over low heat. Cook, stirring, for 3–4 minutes until the sugar has dissolved and the sauce is a golden caramel.

Arrange the raspberries on the cooked pastry rounds and generously brush with the caramel sauce. Bake the tarts for 5–6 minutes until the sauce is bubbling, but the raspberries are still holding their shape. Cool to room temperature.

Place the icing sugar, orange zest and the remaining cream in a bowl and whip until soft peaks form. Serve the raspberry tarts with the orange cream. **Makes 6**

Cinnamon panna cotta with slow-roasted pears

2 cups (500ml) pure (thin)
    cream
½ cup (125ml) milk
3 cinnamon quills
½ tsp ground cinnamon
¼ cup (55g) caster sugar
2 gold-strength gelatine
    leaves*
2 tbs brandy

Slow-roasted pears
4 pears (such as Williams
    or beurre bosc)
6 sage leaves
½ firmly packed cup (110g)
    brown sugar

Combine the cream, milk, cinnamon quills, ground cinnamon and caster sugar in a small saucepan over medium heat. Bring to a simmer, then remove from the heat and leave to infuse for 1 hour.

Soak the gelatine leaves in cold water for 5 minutes to soften. Reheat the cream mixture over low heat. Squeeze excess water from the gelatine, then add the leaves to the hot cream, stirring to dissolve. Stir in the brandy, then strain through a fine sieve into a jug. Pour the mixture into six ½-cup (125ml) ramekins or dariole moulds and chill in the fridge for 4 hours or overnight.

Meanwhile, for the pears, preheat the oven to 160°C. Peel, halve and core the pears, leaving the stems intact. Place the sage leaves, brown sugar and ⅓ cup (80ml) water in a flameproof casserole and stir over low heat until the sugar has dissolved. Add the pears and transfer to the oven. Cook for 3 hours until the pears are very tender. Cool.

When ready to serve, run a knife around the edge of each mould to loosen, then invert the panna cottas onto serving plates. Divide the pears among plates, then drizzle with any remaining pear syrup and serve. **Makes 6**

* Gelatine leaves are from gourmet food shops and selected delis. Always check the packet for setting instructions.

Black Forest Eton mess

680g jar pitted morello
cherries
¼ cup (55g) caster sugar
150g dark chocolate,
chopped
300ml thickened cream
2 tbs icing sugar, sifted
2 tbs kirsch*
6 store-bought meringues

Drain the cherries, reserving the juice. Place the cherry juice and caster sugar in a saucepan over low heat and cook, stirring, until the sugar has dissolved. Increase the heat to medium–high and simmer for 4–5 minutes until reduced to about 1 cup (250ml). Remove from the heat, then add the chocolate and stir until the sauce is smooth. Set aside to cool.

Combine the cream and icing sugar in a bowl and whisk until soft peaks form. Stir in the kirsch and set aside.

Roughly crumble the meringues. Divide half the meringue among 8 serving glasses, then top with half the whipped cream and half the cherries. Repeat the layers, then drizzle over the chocolate cherry sauce and serve. **Serves 8**

* Kirsch is a clear, unsweetened cherry brandy from selected bottleshops.

Plum fool

1kg plums, halved, stones
    removed
Juice of 1 lemon
½ cup (110g) caster sugar
1 vanilla bean, split
    lengthways, seeds scraped
300ml thickened cream
150g ready-made custard
Store-bought meringues,
    to serve
Mint leaves, to decorate

Place the plums, lemon juice, sugar, vanilla bean and seeds and ¼ cup (60ml) water in a saucepan over medium heat. Poach for 10–12 minutes until the plums have softened. Remove with a slotted spoon and set aside.

Return the pan of poaching liquid to medium heat and cook, stirring, for 3–4 minutes until the syrup is reduced by half. Remove from the heat and set aside to cool.

Place the plums in a food processor (reserving a few halves to serve) and process until smooth. Transfer to a large bowl.

Lightly whip the cream, then fold into the plum puree with the custard. Chill the plum fool in the fridge for 30 minutes.

Just before serving, drizzle the plum syrup over the fool. Serve with the reserved plums, meringues and mint leaves. **Serves 6**

Boozy autumn tarts

400g mixed dried fruit (such
  as fig, apple and pear)
100ml brandy
1 cup (220g) caster sugar
2 tbs toasted walnuts,
  crushed
1 egg, lightly beaten
Custard (see page 40),
  to serve

Pastry
2 cups (300g) plain flour
¼ cup (35g) icing sugar,
  plus extra to serve
¼ tsp baking powder
125g chilled unsalted butter,
  chopped
3 tsp lemon juice
1 egg plus 2 extra yolks

Begin this recipe a day ahead.

Place the dried fruit in a bowl with the brandy and just enough boiling water to cover. Allow to cool, then cover and chill overnight.

The next day, for the pastry, place the flour, icing sugar and baking powder in a food processor and whiz to combine. Add the butter and whiz until the mixture resembles breadcrumbs. Add the lemon juice, egg and egg yolks, then whiz until the mixture just comes together. Shape into a ball, then enclose in plastic wrap and chill for 30 minutes.

Preheat oven to 180°C and line a baking tray with baking paper.

Strain the dried fruit, reserving the soaking liquid. Place the soaking liquid and caster sugar in a saucepan over medium-high heat and cook, stirring occasionally, for 5–6 minutes until reduced and syrupy. Roughly chop the fruit and place in a bowl with half the syrup, reserving the remaining syrup. Set aside.

Divide the pastry into 4 portions, then roll out each portion on a lightly floured surface into a 15cm circle. Place the pastry circles on the baking tray, then scatter each with the crushed walnuts, leaving a 3cm border. Pile the soaked fruit on the walnuts, then fold the pastry edge over the filling, pleating and pinching together. Brush the pastry with the beaten egg, then bake for 30 minutes or until the pastry is golden.

Brush the warm tarts with the reserved syrup, dust with the extra icing sugar, then serve immediately with the custard. **Serves 4**

Black-bottom lemon meringue ice cream pie

2 eggs, separated,
  plus 2 extra eggwhites
1 cup (220g) caster sugar
100g unsalted butter,
  softened
Finely grated zest of
  2 lemons
2 tbs lemon juice
300g packet dark chocolate
  shortcrust pastry*
1L (4 cups) good-quality
  vanilla bean ice cream,
  softened at room
  temperature for 20 minutes
Pinch of cream of tartar

You'll need a kitchen blowtorch for this recipe.

Place the egg yolks and ½ cup (110g) sugar in a heatproof bowl set over a saucepan of simmering water (don't let the bowl touch the water). Whisk until well combined. Add the butter and lemon zest and juice, then cook, whisking occasionally, for 10–15 minutes until thick and smooth. Cover the surface closely with a piece of baking paper, set aside to cool, then chill for 30 minutes or until set.

Meanwhile, grease a 24cm-wide, 4cm-deep loose-bottomed tart pan. Roll out the pastry on a lightly floured work surface. Line the pan with the pastry, then chill for 15 minutes.

Preheat the oven to 180°C.

Line the pastry case with baking paper and fill with baking weights or uncooked rice. Bake for 10 minutes, then remove the paper and weights and bake for 5 minutes until the pastry is crisp and dry. Cool.

Spread half the ice cream into the tart shell and dollop with half the lemon curd, then swirl the lemon curd through the ice cream using a skewer. Repeat with the remaining ice cream and lemon curd, then place in the freezer for 3 hours or until firm.

Using electric beaters, whisk the eggwhites and cream of tartar until soft peaks form. Gradually add the remaining sugar, one tablespoon at a time, whisking until firm peaks form. Dollop the meringue mixture over the pie, completely covering the ice cream and swirling with the back of a spoon to create little peaks and folds. Return to the freezer for at least 2 hours. Just before serving, use a kitchen blowtorch to caramelise the meringue. Cut into slices and serve immediately. **Serves 6–8**

* We used Careme Dark Chocolate Shortcrust Pastry. For stockists, visit: caremepastry.com.

Mango and chilli upside-down cakes

250g golden syrup

1 long red chilli, seeds
removed, chopped

Finely grated zest of 1 lime

1 mango, peeled, thinly sliced

225g unsalted butter,
softened

1 cup (220g) caster sugar

4 eggs

1 tsp vanilla extract

1½ cups (225g) self-raising
flour, sifted

1–2 tbs milk

Preheat the oven to 170°C. Grease the base and sides of a 6-hole (185ml) Texas muffin pan and line with baking paper.

Place the golden syrup, chilli and lime zest in a saucepan and warm gently over medium-low heat for 1–2 minutes. Place 1 tablespoon of the chilli syrup in the base of each muffin hole, reserving the rest to serve. Cover the base with slices of mango, slightly overlapping.

Place the butter and sugar in the bowl of an electric mixer and beat until thick and pale. Add the eggs one at a time, beating well after each addition. Add the vanilla, then fold in the flour. Stir in enough milk to give a soft dropping consistency.

Divide the cake batter among the muffin holes, then bake for 20–25 minutes until a skewer inserted in the centre comes out clean. Allow to stand in the pans for 2 minutes before inverting the muffin pan onto a wire rack to cool completely. (At this stage, leave the muffin pan over the cakes and sit a chopping board on top to help flatten the base of the cakes so they sit well for presentation.)

When the cakes have cooled, lift off the pan and remove the baking paper. Rewarm the remaining chilli syrup and drizzle over each cake. You can serve the cakes at room temperature or gently rewarmed in a low oven or microwave. **Makes 6**

Swedish apple cake

2 eggs
250g caster sugar
100g unsalted butter,
    chopped
150ml milk
1 tsp vanilla extract
175g self-raising flour, sifted
4 small Granny Smith apples,
    peeled, cored, sliced 1cm
    thick
Pure (thin) cream or vanilla
    ice cream, to serve

Preheat the oven to 180°C. Grease a 24cm springform cake pan or loose-bottomed tart pan.

Place the eggs in a bowl with 200g sugar and use a hand whisk to combine well.

Place the butter, milk and vanilla in a saucepan over medium-low heat and cook, stirring, until the butter has melted.

Slowly whisk the milk mixture into the egg mixture, then fold in the flour until combined.

Lay half the apple slices in the base of the pan. Carefully pour in the batter, then arrange the remaining apple slices on top. Sprinkle with the remaining 50g sugar, then bake for 25 minutes or until puffed and golden. Allow to cool slightly in the pan, then transfer to a platter. Serve warm with the cream or ice cream. **Serves 6**

Moroccan apple pies with rose custard

4 green apples, peeled,
   cored, cut into 2cm pieces
1 tsp finely grated lemon zest
2 tbs lemon juice
1 vanilla bean, split
   lengthways, seeds scraped
½ cup (110g) caster sugar
1 tsp Fragrant Sweet Spices
   blend* or ground cinnamon
50g sultanas
1 tsp cornflour
4 sheets filo pastry
80g unsalted butter, melted,
   cooled
2 tbs dried edible rose
   petals*
Icing sugar, to dust

Rose custard
1 qty warm creme anglaise
   (see page 52)
2 tbs rosewater*
Rose food colouring

Preheat the oven to 200°C and grease 6 holes of a 12-hole medium muffin pan.

Place the apple, lemon zest and juice, vanilla bean and seeds, caster sugar, spices, sultanas and 2 tablespoons water in a saucepan over low heat. Cover and cook for 6 minutes or until the apple is tender. Remove from the heat and allow to cool. When cool, mix the cornflour with 2 teaspoons hot water, then stir into the apple mixture.

Place the filo sheets on top of each other, then slice into six 15cm squares to make 24 squares in total. Leaving the remaining pastry covered with a damp tea towel as you work, brush 4 squares with the melted butter, then place in a muffin hole, positioning each layer at an angle to fill the hole entirely, leaving the pastry overhanging the edges. Repeat with the remaining pastry to make 6 pie cases. Divide the apple filling among the pie cases, then fold in the sides to enclose. Brush the tops of the pies with a little more butter, then bake for 15–20 minutes until the pastry is golden.

Meanwhile, for the custard, mix the warm creme anglaise with the rosewater and 1–2 drops of food colouring to taste.

Remove the pies from the oven, brush with the remaining butter and scatter with the dried rose petals. Leave to cool slightly, then transfer to serving plates, dust with the icing sugar and serve with the rose custard. **Makes 6**

* Fragrant Sweet Spices and dried edible rose petals are from gourmet food shops and herbies.com.au. Rosewater is from Middle Eastern and gourmet food shops.

Yoghurt cake with rose-scented berries

1⅓ cups (200g) self-raising
  flour
1 cup (125g) almond meal
150g caster sugar
1 tsp baking powder
2 eggs, lightly beaten
250g thick Greek-style
  yoghurt
150ml sunflower oil
Finely grated zest of 1 small
  lemon
Icing sugar, to dust

Rose-scented berries
175g caster sugar
Juice of 1 lemon
1 tbs rosewater*
500g fresh or frozen mixed
  berries

Preheat the oven to 180°C. Grease a 20cm springform cake pan and line the base with baking paper.

Sift the flour into a bowl and add the almond meal, sugar and baking powder.

Gently whisk the egg, yoghurt, oil and zest in a separate bowl, then add to the dry ingredients and stir using a wooden spoon until well combined. Pour into the cake pan and smooth the top. Bake for 30 minutes or until a skewer inserted in the centre comes out clean. Cool slightly, then remove from the pan and place on a wire rack to cool completely.

Meanwhile, for the rose-scented berries, place the sugar, lemon juice and 1 cup (250ml) water in a saucepan and bring to the boil, stirring to dissolve the sugar. Decrease the heat to low and simmer, without stirring, for 5 minutes until syrupy. Leave to cool, then stir in the rosewater and berries.

Just before serving, spoon some of the berries and syrup over the cake and dust with the icing sugar. Serve with the remaining berries. **Serves 6–8**

* Rosewater is available from Middle Eastern shops and selected supermarkets.

Ricotta and Marsala cheesecake

100g raisins

⅓ cup (80ml) Marsala*

150g amaretti (Italian almond
  biscuits)*

150g digestive biscuits

150g unsalted butter, melted,
  cooled

500g ricotta

1 cup (250g) mascarpone

150ml thickened cream

5 eggs

1¼ cups (275g) caster sugar

1 tbs plain flour

Finely grated zest and juice
  of 1 lemon

Icing sugar, to dust

Preheat oven to 180°C. Grease and line a 22cm springform cake pan.

Place the raisins and Marsala in a saucepan over medium heat
and bring to a simmer. Remove from the heat and set aside to cool.

Place the biscuits and butter in a food processor and whiz to fine
crumbs. Press into the base of the cake pan and chill for 15 minutes.
Bake for 10 minutes until just set and golden. Allow to cool.

Meanwhile, place the ricotta, mascarpone, cream, eggs, caster
sugar, flour and lemon zest and juice in a food processor and whiz
until smooth.

Strain the raisins, reserving the Marsala. Stir the Marsala
through the cheese mixture.

Pour the cheese mixture onto the biscuit base, then sprinkle
the raisins over the top (the raisins will sink to the bottom as the
cake cooks). Bake for 1¼ hours or until the top is golden and
the cake has a gentle wobble. Cool to room temperature in the
pan, then refrigerate and chill completely.

Dust with the icing sugar, cut into slices and serve. **Serves 6–8**

* Marsala is an Italian fortified wine from bottle shops. Amaretti are
from delis and gourmet food shops.

Mille-feuille with praline cream, raspberries and mango

2 sheets frozen puff
   pastry, thawed
½ cup (70g) icing sugar, sifted
½ cup (110g) caster sugar
¼ cup (40g) blanched
   almonds, toasted
1 cup (250g) mascarpone
2 x 125g punnets raspberries
1 small mango, sliced

Preheat the oven to 200°C. Line 2 baking trays with baking paper and lightly grease another baking tray.

Cut the pastry into 24 rectangles, each measuring 12cm x 4cm. Divide between the 2 lined baking trays and dust with half the icing sugar. Lay baking paper sheets over the pastry and place heavy baking trays on top to weigh down. Bake for 25 minutes or until the pastry is golden. Cool.

Meanwhile, place the caster sugar with 2 tablespoons water in a saucepan and cook over low heat, swirling the pan occasionally, until the sugar has dissolved. Increase the heat to medium–high and cook for a further 3–4 minutes, swirling the pan occasionally, until a golden caramel. Remove from the heat and add the almonds, then pour onto the greased baking tray. Allow to cool.

When the praline has set, break into shards, place in a food processor and whiz until coarsely ground. Reserve 1 tablespoon praline, then combine the remaining praline with the mascarpone. Set aside.

Dust half the cooked pastry rectangles with the remaining icing sugar. Carefully heat a metal skewer over an open flame until very hot, then press the skewer onto the sugar-dusted pastry in a crisscross pattern – you will need to reheat the skewer each time.

To assemble, top the undusted pastry rectangles with the mascarpone mixture, a few raspberries and a slice of mango, then carefully top with the sugar-dusted pastry rectangles. Decorate with any remaining raspberries and the reserved praline to serve.

Makes 12

Apple galette

6 Granny Smith apples

2 tbs lemon juice

375g block frozen puff pastry,
   thawed

100g unsalted butter,
   chopped

185g caster sugar

Cream or vanilla ice cream,
   to serve

Preheat the oven to 180°C. Line a baking tray or pizza tray with baking paper.

Peel and core the apples, then slice very thinly (a mandoline slicer is ideal). Gently toss with the lemon juice to prevent the slices from discolouring.

On a lightly floured surface, roll out the pastry to 5mm thick and trim into a neat 28cm circle. Place on the lined tray. Arrange the apple slices in overlapping circles – with each slice overlapping to ensure that they all fit on the base. Dot with the butter and sprinkle with half the sugar. Cover with another sheet of baking paper and a second heavy baking tray. Bake for 35 minutes.

Gently remove the top tray and baking paper (being careful of the hot juices). Sprinkle with the remaining sugar, then return to the oven, uncovered, for a further 10–15 minutes until well caramelised. Slice the galette and serve warm with the cream or ice cream.

Serves 4–6

Gin and tonic tart

4 eggs
¾ cup (165g) caster sugar
1 tbs finely grated lemon zest
¾ cup (185ml) strained
   lemon juice
150ml thickened cream
¼ cup (60ml) gin

Pastry
200g plain flour, sifted
¼ cup (35g) icing sugar, sifted
75g chilled unsalted butter,
   chopped
2 tsp lemon zest
1 egg yolk
¼ cup (60ml) chilled tonic
   water

Gin and tonic syrup
150g caster sugar
1 cup (250ml) tonic water
Very thinly pared zest
   and juice of 2 lemons
¼ cup (60ml) gin
5 juniper berries*, lightly
   bruised

For the pastry, place the flour, icing sugar, butter and lemon zest in a food processor and whiz until the mixture resembles fine crumbs. Add the egg yolk and tonic water and process until the mixture comes together in a smooth ball. Enclose in plastic wrap and chill for 30 minutes.

Preheat oven to 180°C. Grease a 23cm loose-bottomed tart pan.

Roll out the pastry on a lightly floured surface until 5mm thick, then use it to line the tart pan. Chill for 15 minutes.

Line the pastry case with baking paper and fill with baking weights or uncooked rice. Bake for 10 minutes, then remove the paper and weights and bake for a further 5 minutes or until the pastry is golden and dry. Allow to cool.

Whisk the eggs, sugar, lemon zest and juice, cream and gin together until combined. Pour the filling into the tart shell and bake for 20–25 minutes until just set.

Meanwhile, for the syrup, place the sugar, tonic water and lemon juice in a saucepan over low heat, stirring to dissolve the sugar. Add the gin and juniper berries and simmer for 5–10 minutes until slightly thickened. Blanch the lemon zest in boiling water for 2 minutes, drain, then add to the syrup. Simmer for a further 5 minutes, then cool.

Remove the juniper berries from the gin and tonic syrup, then drizzle the syrup over the tart and serve. **Serves 8–10**

* Juniper berries are from supermarkets and delis.

Ginger cakes with chilli icing

175g unsalted butter, softened

175g caster sugar

3 eggs

1⅔ cups (250g) self-raising flour, sifted

1 tsp ground ginger

Pinch of cayenne pepper

100g preserved ginger in syrup*, finely chopped, plus extra ⅓ cup (80ml) syrup

1 long red chilli, seeds removed, finely chopped

1 cup (150g) icing sugar, sifted

Preheat the oven to 180°C. Grease a 12-hole muffin pan.

Beat the butter and caster sugar in an electric mixer until thick and pale. Add the eggs, one at a time, beating well after each addition. Fold in the flour and spices, then stir in most of the chopped ginger and 2 tablespoons extra ginger syrup. Spoon into the muffin holes and bake for 20 minutes or until golden and a skewer inserted in the centre comes out clean. Cool slightly in the pan, then invert onto a wire rack and cool completely.

Meanwhile, soak the chilli in 1 tablespoon boiling water for 15 minutes. Combine the chilli and soaking liquid with the remaining 2 tablespoons ginger syrup. Add the icing sugar and stir until a soft icing.

Drizzle the chilli icing over the cooled cakes, then decorate with the remaining chopped ginger. **Makes 12**

* Preserved ginger in syrup is from Asian food shops and selected supermarkets.

Easy baklava

500g unsalted mixed nuts
   (such as walnuts, pistachios
   and almonds)
250g honey
250g caster sugar
Zest and juice of 2 oranges
2 cardamom pods, smashed
1 cinnamon quill
12 sheets filo pastry
80g unsalted butter, melted
Vanilla ice cream, to serve

Preheat the oven to 200°C. Spread the nuts on a baking tray and toast for 5 minutes. Cool slightly, then finely chop in a food processor and set aside.

Meanwhile, combine the honey, sugar, orange zest and juice, cardamom, cinnamon and 300ml water in a saucepan over medium heat. Boil for 5 minutes or until syrupy, then allow to cool.

Lay 1 sheet of filo pastry on a bench and brush with the butter. Cover with another filo sheet and brush with more butter. Sprinkle all over with a layer of nuts, leaving a 1cm border. Fold in the 2 shorter ends and roll quite tightly into a log. Place seam-side down on a greased baking tray, then repeat with the remaining pastry, butter and nuts to make 6 rolls. Bake for 5–6 minutes or until golden brown.

Cool the rolls slightly, then cut into pieces. Place in a shallow dish, pour over the cooled syrup, then stand for at least 1 hour.

Serve with the ice cream, drizzled with some of the syrup.

Serves 6

Chocolate-swirl meringues with glazed strawberries

4 eggwhites
1 cup (220g) caster sugar
2 tsp cornflour
1 tsp white wine vinegar
1 tbs cocoa powder
⅓ cup (110g) good-quality
   strawberry jam
250g punnet strawberries,
   hulled, halved
300ml thickened cream
2 tbs icing sugar, sifted
1 vanilla bean, split
   lengthways, seeds scraped

Preheat the oven to 140°C. Line a large baking tray with baking paper.

Place the eggwhites and caster sugar in a heatproof bowl set over a saucepan of barely simmering water (don't let the bowl touch the water), stirring until the sugar has dissolved. Transfer the mixture to an electric mixer and whisk until firm peaks form. Carefully fold in the cornflour and vinegar with a metal spoon until just combined. Sift the cocoa over the eggwhite mixture and carefully stir through with the metal spoon until you have lovely chocolate swirls.

Spoon the mixture into 6 large rounds on the prepared tray, making a slight indent in the centre of each with the back of the spoon. Place in the oven and immediately reduce the temperature to 120°C. Bake for 1¼ hours or until crisp and dry. Switch the oven off and leave the door slightly ajar. Allow the meringues to cool completely in the oven.

Meanwhile, place the jam and ¼ cup (60ml) cold water in a saucepan over low heat and stir gently until the jam is melted and syrupy. Remove from the heat, then stir through the strawberries. Allow to cool.

Whisk the cream with the icing sugar and vanilla seeds until soft peaks form. Keep chilled until ready to serve.

To serve, top the meringues with the whipped cream and spoon over the glazed strawberries and a little syrup. **Serves 6**

Grand Marnier crepe layer cake

600ml thickened cream

¾ cup (120g) icing sugar, plus
extra to dust

2 tsp finely grated orange
zest, plus pared zest of
2 oranges

1 tsp vanilla extract

¾ cup (185ml) Grand Marnier

250g caster sugar

Crepes

2 cups (300g) plain flour

1 tsp baking powder

2 tbs pure icing sugar

4 eggs

450ml milk

1 cup (250ml) pure (thin)
cream

½ tsp vanilla extract

100g unsalted butter, melted,
cooled

For the crepes, whiz all ingredients except butter in a processor until smooth, pour into a jug and stand for 30 minutes at room temperature. Heat a 20cm crepe pan or small frypan over medium heat and brush with a little melted butter. Add ¼ cup (60ml) crepe batter and swirl to coat the base of the pan. Cook for 2 minutes each side until just golden. Repeat with the remaining batter to make about 30 crepes, stacking with baking paper between the layers. Set aside.

Use electric beaters to whisk the cream, icing sugar, finely grated zest, vanilla and ¼ cup (60ml) of the Grand Marnier until stiff peaks form.

Grease a 20cm springform cake pan and line the base with baking paper. Layer the crepes, spreading each with a thin layer of cream mixture and finishing with a crepe. Cover and chill for at least 4 hours until set.

Meanwhile, to make an orange sauce, place caster sugar and 100ml water in a pan over low heat and stir to dissolve sugar. Increase the heat to medium and simmer, not stirring, for 6–8 minutes until a golden toffee colour (watch carefully, as it burns easily). Remove from heat and carefully add 150ml boiling water (it may spit) and pared zest. Return to medium-low heat and stir for 2–3 minutes until thickened. Add remaining ½ cup (125ml) Grand Marnier and swirl to combine. Cool.

Transfer the chilled cake to a serving platter, then cut into slices and serve drizzled with some of the orange sauce and dusted with the extra icing sugar. **Serves 8–10**

Classic vanilla cheesecake

300g chocolate shortbread
   biscuits*
70g unsalted butter, melted
750g cream cheese
150g thickened cream
1 vanilla bean, split
   lengthways, seeds scraped
2 eggs plus 8 egg yolks
240g caster sugar
600ml sour cream
Raspberries or other seasonal
   berries, and mint leaves, to
   serve
1 cup (250ml) chocolate
   sauce, to serve

Chocolate sauce
185g brown sugar
60g unsalted butter
300ml pure (thin) cream
100g dark chocolate (70%),
   chopped

To make the chocolate sauce, place the sugar, butter and cream in a pan over medium heat. Bring to the boil, then remove from the heat. Add the chocolate and stir until melted. Cool.

Preheat the oven to 160°C. Line a 20cm x 30cm lamington pan with baking paper.

Place the biscuits in a food processor and process to fine crumbs, then add the butter and pulse until just combined.

Press the biscuit mixture into the base of the prepared pan, then bake for 10 minutes. Allow to cool completely.

Reduce the oven to 110°C.

Place the cream cheese, cream, vanilla seeds, eggs, egg yolks and 200g sugar in the cleaned food processor and process until smooth. Pour the cream mixture over the biscuit base and bake for 1 hour 15 minutes or until just set.

Meanwhile, place the sour cream and remaining 40g sugar in the food processor and process until completely smooth. Pour the sour cream mixture over the cheesecake, then return to the oven for a further 15 minutes. The cheesecake will still have a slight wobble. Turn off the heat and allow the cheesecake to cool in the oven with the door ajar. Once cool, chill for 3 hours or overnight until set.

Slice the cheesecake into 12 bars and serve with the berries and mint or chocolate sauce, or both. **Serves 12**

* We used Duchy Originals biscuits, available from gourmet food shops. Substitute plain shortbread and 1 tablespoon good-quality (Dutch) cocoa powder.

Honey pots de creme

½ cup (180g) honey,
   plus extra to serve
300ml pure (thin) cream
1 cup (250ml) milk
2 tbs caster sugar
1 vanilla bean, split
   lengthways, seeds scraped
1 egg, plus 5 egg yolks
Honeycomb and melted dark
   chocolate, to serve

Preheat the oven to 160°C.

Place the honey, cream and milk in a saucepan over medium heat, stirring to combine. Bring to just below boiling point, then remove from the heat and set aside.

Meanwhile, beat the sugar, vanilla seeds, egg and egg yolks with electric beaters until thick and pale. Pour the milk mixture into the egg mixture and gently stir to combine, trying not to create too much froth. Strain the mixture into a jug, then pour into six ¾ cup (185ml) ramekins (or ovenproof jars).

Place the ramekins in a deep roasting pan and pour enough boiling water into the pan to come halfway up the sides of the ramekins. Bake for 50–60 minutes until set but with a slight wobble. Allow to cool completely, then chill for 1 hour.

Drizzle the honey pots with the extra honey and serve with the honeycomb dipped in melted chocolate. **Serves 6**

Persian trifle

2 tbs Cointreau or other
   orange liqueur
Finely grated zest and juice
   of 1 orange
Finely grated zest and juice
   of 1 lemon
½ cup (75g) icing sugar, sifted
300g store-bought plain
   sponge cake cut into
   2cm pieces
12 pieces (240g) Turkish
   delight, chopped
1 tbs rosewater*
300ml carton thick custard
300ml thickened cream
250g thick Greek-style
   yoghurt
Juice and seeds of
   1 pomegranate* (optional)
Edible dried rose petals*
   and chopped unsalted
   pistachios (optional),
   to serve

Place the Cointreau, citrus zest and juice, and ¼ cup (35g) icing sugar in a bowl, stirring until the sugar dissolves. Set aside.

Divide the sponge cake among six 1½ cup (375ml) serving dishes, drizzle with the Cointreau mixture, then scatter over half the Turkish delight. Stir the rosewater into the custard, then pour into the serving dishes.

Whip the cream and the remaining icing sugar together until soft peaks form, then fold through the yoghurt. Dollop over the custard and chill for at least 6 hours.

If desired, drizzle the trifles with the pomegranate juice and decorate with the pomegranate seeds, rose petals and pistachios. Serve the trifles topped with the remaining Turkish delight.

Serves 6

* Rosewater and dried rose petals are from Middle Eastern food shops. Pomegranates are available in season from greengrocers and selected supermarkets.

Coconut creme caramel

500g caster sugar
400ml can coconut milk
300ml pure (thin) cream
300ml milk
2 eggs plus 7 egg yolks
Seasonal fruit, to serve

Begin this recipe a day ahead.

Preheat the oven to 160°C.

Place 300g sugar and 2 tablespoons cold water in a saucepan over medium-low heat, stirring until the sugar dissolves. Increase the heat to medium and cook, swirling the pan occasionally, for 5–6 minutes until a golden caramel. Pour into a 20cm round cake pan (not springform).

Place the coconut milk, cream, milk and remaining 200g sugar in a saucepan over medium heat. Bring to just below boiling point, then remove from the heat.

Lightly beat the eggs and egg yolks together in a large bowl, then pour the warm milk mixture into the eggs, gently whisking to combine. Strain into a jug, then pour over the caramel.

Place the cake pan in a deep roasting pan. Fill the roasting pan with enough boiling water to come halfway up the side of the cake pan. Loosely cover the roasting pan with foil, then bake for 1 hour – the creme caramel should still have a slight wobble, but will firm on cooling. Cool in the pan, then chill overnight.

To unmould the creme caramel, dip the base of the cake pan briefly in hot water, then carefully invert the creme caramel onto a plate. Cut into slices and serve with the seasonal fruit. **Serves 6**

Simple summer pudding

600g frozen mixed berries
½ cup (110g) caster sugar
10 slices white bread, crusts
   removed, halved into
   triangles
Pure (thin) cream, to serve

Place the fruit in a saucepan with the sugar and ¼ cup (60ml) water and bring to the boil over medium heat. Reduce the heat to low and simmer for 3–4 minutes until the sugar dissolves and the fruit starts to give off some of its juice.

Layer one-third of the bread in a 1-litre (4-cup) serving dish, cutting pieces to fit, if necessary. Using a slotted spoon, top the bread with half the berry mixture. Repeat with another layer of bread and fruit, then finish with the final layer of bread. Pour the liquid remaining in the pan over the bread, pressing down well. Cover and chill for at least 30 minutes, then serve drizzled with the cream. **Serves 6**

White chocolate brulee

300ml thickened cream
100ml milk
1 vanilla bean, split
    lengthways, seeds scraped
200g white chocolate,
    chopped
4 egg yolks, beaten
¼ cup (55g) caster sugar

Blueberry compote
¼ cup (55g) caster sugar
200g blueberries
Juice of 1 lime

Place the cream, milk and vanilla bean and seeds in a saucepan over medium-low heat and bring to just below boiling point. Place the chocolate in a bowl and pour over the hot cream mixture, then stir for 2 minutes until smooth. Add the egg yolks and return to very low heat, stirring, for 2–3 minutes until slightly thickened. Strain into a jug, then pour into four 200ml glasses or ramekins and chill until set.

Meanwhile, for the blueberry compote, place the sugar and 2 tablespoons water in a saucepan over low heat and stir until the sugar dissolves. Increase the heat to medium and simmer for 1–2 minutes until syrupy. Add the blueberries and lime juice and cook for about 2 minutes until they release their juices. Chill in the fridge until ready to serve.

Sprinkle the creams with the caster sugar and use a kitchen blowtorch to brulee the tops. Alternatively, heat a grill to high and cook until the sugar melts and caramelises. Serve immediately, topped with the blueberry compote. **Serves 4**

Turkish delight cheesecake

300g shortbread
   or digestive biscuits
¼ cup (25g) cocoa powder,
   sifted
80g unsalted butter, melted
8 gold-strength
   gelatine leaves
1kg cream cheese,
   at room temperature
1¼ cups (275g) caster sugar
⅓ cup (80ml) milk
300ml thickened cream
¼ cup (60ml) rosewater
2 x 250g punnets
   strawberries, hulled, halved

Grease a 22cm springform cake pan.

Place the biscuits and cocoa in a food processor and whiz to fine crumbs. Add the butter and pulse to combine. Press the mixture into the cake pan, then chill.

Soak 5 gelatine leaves in cold water for 5 minutes.

Meanwhile, place the cream cheese and ¾ cup (165g) sugar in the cleaned food processor and whiz until smooth. Place the milk in a saucepan over medium-high heat and bring to just below boiling point. Squeeze excess water from the gelatine, then add the gelatine to the milk, stirring until the gelatine has dissolved. Cool slightly, then add to the cream cheese mixture in the food processor and whiz to combine. Transfer to a bowl.

Beat the cream with electric beaters until soft peaks form, then fold the cream into the cream cheese mixture with 1 tablespoon rosewater. Pour the filling over the biscuit base and gently tap the pan on the bench to dispel any air pockets. Cover in plastic wrap and chill for 4 hours or until the filling is set.

Place the strawberries and the remaining sugar in a heatproof bowl with ½ cup (125ml) water, stirring to dissolve the sugar. Cover the bowl tightly with foil and place over a saucepan of simmering water (don't let the bowl touch the water). Simmer for 20 minutes, topping up the pan with more water if needed, until the strawberries are very soft.

Soak the remaining 3 gelatine leaves in cold water for 5 minutes.

Pass the strawberry mixture through a fine sieve into a bowl – don't press down on the fruit, or the jelly will be cloudy. While the juice is warm, squeeze excess water from the gelatine, then stir the gelatine into the juice until dissolved. Stir in the remaining rosewater. Cool completely, then place in the fridge for 15 minutes until just starting to thicken. Pour the strawberry jelly over the cheesecake, then return to the fridge for 3–4 hours until completely set. **Serves 8-10**

Cremets with caramel oranges

200g cream cheese
¼ cup (55g) caster sugar
2 cups (500ml) pure (thin)
    cream
1 vanilla bean, split
    lengthways, seeds scraped

Caramel oranges
4 oranges
1½ cups (330g) caster sugar
3 star anise
2 cinnamon quills

Cut 6 squares of muslin, cheesecloth or plastic wrap, then use to line 6 teacups or 150ml dariole moulds, leaving plenty overhanging the sides.

Place the cream cheese and sugar in a bowl and beat with electric beaters until smooth. Slowly add the cream, beating constantly, then stir in the vanilla seeds to combine. Press the cream cheese mixture into the cups or moulds, then cover with the overhanging cloth or wrap. Chill for at least 2 hours or overnight until firm.

For the oranges, cut away all the skin and white pith from the fruit, then slice thinly into rounds. Arrange the orange slices in a heatproof dish in a single layer. Combine the sugar and 1½ cups (375ml) water in a saucepan over low heat, stirring to dissolve the sugar. Add the spices and bring to the boil over medium-high heat. Reduce heat to medium, then simmer, without stirring, for 10–15 minutes until you have a golden caramel, brushing down the sides of the pan with a wet pastry brush to prevent crystals forming. Pour the hot caramel over the oranges and leave at room temperature for 1–2 hours – the caramel will start to break down into a delicious sauce with some crunchy shards of toffee.

To serve, dip the base of each mould in warm water and carefully turn out onto serving plates. Remove the cloth or wrap and serve with the caramel oranges. **Serves 6**

Blackberry frozen yoghurt with berry caramel

150g fresh or frozen, thawed
    blackberries
395g can sweetened
    condensed milk
500g thick Greek-style
    yoghurt

Berry caramel
1 cup (220g) caster sugar
100g fresh or frozen, thawed
    blackberries
1 tsp vanilla extract

Place the blackberries in a food processor and whiz until a smooth puree. Stir in the condensed milk and yoghurt, then transfer to an ice-cream machine and churn according to the manufacturer's instructions. (Alternatively, pour the mixture into a shallow container and freeze for 2 hours or until frozen at the edges. Remove from the freezer and beat with electric beaters, then return to the freezer. Repeat the process 2–3 times.) Freeze for 3–4 hours until firm.

Meanwhile, for the blackberry caramel, place the sugar and 2 tablespoons water in a saucepan over low heat, stirring until the sugar dissolves. Increase the heat to medium–high and cook, swirling the pan occasionally, for a further 3–4 minutes until a light caramel. Cool slightly. Place the blackberries and vanilla in the cleaned food processor and whiz until smooth, then stir into the caramel and allow to cool completely.

Serve the frozen blackberry yoghurt drizzled with the berry caramel. **Serves 6–8**

Choc-ice meringues with hot white chocolate sauce

200g good-quality dark
chocolate, chopped
50ml freshly brewed espresso
coffee
400g store-bought custard
300ml thickened cream
4 store-bought meringue
nests
Cocoa powder, to dust

White chocolate sauce
75g white chocolate,
chopped
100ml pure (thin) cream

Place the chocolate and coffee in a heatproof bowl over a saucepan of simmering water (don't let the bowl touch the water) and stir until melted and smooth. Remove from the heat.

In a separate bowl, combine the custard and cream, then stir in the chocolate mixture. Churn in an ice-cream machine following the manufacturer's directions. (Alternatively, pour the mixture into a shallow container and freeze for 2–3 hours until frozen at the edges. Remove from the freezer and beat with electric beaters, then refreeze. Repeat this process two or three times.)

Just before serving, make the chocolate sauce. Place the chocolate and cream in a heatproof bowl over a saucepan of simmering water (don't let the bowl touch the water) and stir until melted and smooth. Keep warm.

Place the meringues on serving plates, then top each with a scoop of the chocolate ice cream. Dust with the cocoa and drizzle with the warm chocolate sauce. **Serves 4**

Pistachio and date kulfi

⅔ cup (100g) unsalted
   pistachio kernels
395g can sweetened
   condensed milk
300ml thickened cream
125g fresh pitted dates,
   finely chopped
1 tbs orange blossom water*
3 oranges
½ cup (110g) caster sugar

Line six 150ml dariole moulds with plastic wrap, leaving some overhanging the sides.

Process the pistachios and condensed milk in a food processor until the nuts are finely chopped and you have a coarse paste.

Lightly whip the cream in a large bowl, then fold in the condensed milk mixture, dates and orange blossom water.

Divide the mixture among the moulds, then cover with the overhanging plastic wrap and freeze for at least 6 hours or overnight until firm.

Zest the rind of 1 orange using a zester. Place in a saucepan with the juice of 2 oranges, the caster sugar and ½ cup (125ml) water. Stir over low heat to dissolve the sugar, then simmer for 5 minutes until the syrup has thickened. Set aside to cool.

When ready to serve, peel the remaining orange, then slice the flesh into rounds. Place on a serving plate and drizzle with some of the candied rind and syrup. Turn out the kulfi onto serving plates, then drizzle with the remaining rind and syrup and serve with the orange slices. **Serves 6**

* Fresh dates are from greengrocers. Orange blossom water is available from supermarkets.

Peanut butter ice cream with caramel popcorn brittle

1L good-quality vanilla ice
cream, softened

1 cup (280g) crunchy peanut
butter

1 cup (220g) caster sugar

20g unsalted butter

100g packet microwave
popcorn, cooked to
instructions

⅔ cup (100g) salted peanuts,
crushed

½ tsp sea salt

Caramel sauce (see page 56),
to serve

Place the ice cream and peanut butter in a food processor and pulse to combine. Pour into a lined 1-litre (4-cup) terrine mould or loaf pan and freeze for at least 4 hours or until firm.

Place the sugar and 100ml water in a saucepan over low heat, bring to a simmer and stir to dissolve the sugar. Cook for 6–8 minutes, watching carefully, until it becomes a light caramel colour. Add the butter, popcorn and peanuts, stirring quickly to coat (the mixture will seize, but continue cooking over medium-low heat until the caramel is smooth again), then stir in sea salt.

Spread the mixture onto a sheet of baking paper. When cool enough to handle, break the caramel popcorn into small shards.

Turn out the ice cream and slice into wedges. Serve with the popcorn shards, drizzled with the caramel sauce. **Serves 6–8**

Ice-cream pie

400g chocolate cream
   biscuits (such as Oreos)
120g unsalted butter, melted
150ml dry white wine
2 tbs brandy
Finely grated zest and juice
   of 2 lemons
Finely grated zest of
   1 orange
1 tsp vanilla extract
⅓ cup (70g) caster sugar
500ml thickened cream
2 mangoes

Line the base of a 22cm loose-bottomed tart pan with baking paper.

Pulse the biscuits to fine crumbs in a food processor. Add the melted butter and pulse briefly to combine. Press the crumb mixture well into the base and side of the tart pan. Chill while you make the filling.

Clean the food processor, then add the wine, brandy, citrus zest and juice, vanilla and sugar. Process to combine and dissolve the sugar, then add the cream with the motor running and process for about 1 minute until the mixture is thick and well combined.

Pour the mixture into the tart shell and freeze for at least 3 hours until firm. Transfer the tart to the fridge about 30 minutes before serving to soften slightly.

Meanwhile, clean the food processor again and blend the mango flesh to a smooth puree.

When ready to serve, remove the tart from the pan and place on a platter. Drizzle with some of the puree, then slice and serve with the remaining puree on the side. **Serves 6–8**

Blanco y negro

2 cups (500ml) milk
150ml thickened cream
150g caster sugar
Grated zest of 1 lemon
2 cinnamon quills
1 tbs brandy
3 eggwhites
Hot espresso coffee, to serve
Almond praline (optional),
   to serve

Place the milk, cream and 100g sugar in a saucepan over medium heat with the lemon zest and cinnamon quills. Bring to just below boiling point, then remove from the heat and stand for 40 minutes to infuse. Strain through a sieve into a large bowl, discarding solids, then stir in the brandy.

In a separate bowl, use electric beaters to whisk the eggwhites and remaining 50g sugar until stiff peaks form. Gently fold into the milk mixture.

Pour the mixture into a shallow container and freeze for 2–3 hours until frozen at the edges. Remove from the freezer and beat with electric beaters, then refreeze. Repeat this process two or three times. (Alternatively, churn in an ice-cream machine following the manufacturer's directions.)

When ready to serve, place a large scoop of ice cream in four serving glasses. Pour a shot of espresso coffee over each one and serve with the praline, if desired. **Serves 4**

Index

ABC Books

The ABC 'Wave' device is a trademark of the Australian Broadcasting Corporation and is used under licence by HarperCollins*Publishers* Australia. The *delicious.* trademark is used under licence from the Australian Broadcasting Corporation and NewsLifeMedia.

delicious. Indulge comprises recipes and photographs originally published in *delicious. Faking It* (2008), *delicious. Quick Smart Cook* (2009), *delicious. More Please* (2010), *delicious. Simply the Best* (2011) and *delicious. Home Cooking* (2012)

First published in Australia in 2014
by HarperCollins*Publishers* Australia Pty Limited
ABN 36 009 913 517
harpercollins.com.au

Copyright © NewsLifeMedia 2014

HarperCollins*Publishers*
Level 13, 201 Elizabeth Street, Sydney NSW 2000, Australia
Unit D1, 63 Apollo Drive, Rosedale, Auckland 0632 New Zealand
A 53, Sector 57, Noida, UP, India
1 London Bridge Street, London SE1 9GF, United Kingdom
2 Bloor Street East, 20th floor, Toronto, Ontario M4W 1A8, Canada
195 Broadway, New York, NY 10007, USA

National Library of Australia Cataloguing-in-Publication data:
Little, Valli, author.
Delicious: indulge / Valli Little.
  ISBN: 978 0 7333 3337 8 (paperback)
  Cooking.
  Confectionery.
  Desserts.
  Cake.
641.8653

Photography by Brett Stevens, Ian Wallace
Styling by David Morgan, Louise Pickford
Cover and internal design by Hazel Lam, HarperCollins Design Studio
Typesetting by Judi Rowe, Agave Creative Group
Colour reproduction by Graphic Print Group, Adelaide, SA

Printed and bound in China by RR Donnelley

7 6 5 4   15 16 17 18